Midnight Motel

shilpi kulshrestha

BookLeaf Publishing

India | USA | UK

Presentation by *BookLeaf Publishing*

Web: www.bookleafpub.com

E-mail: info@bookleafpub.com

ISBN: 9789363312005

First edition 2024

PREFACE

Limerence

you wanna come to my motel, honey?

Heavy Boxes
Stored away
Little memories
Weighing me down
And now I don't know
How to get up again.

you wanna hold me down?

Touching toes
I giggle
You swear
On
My
Little
Finger
To always
Eat my
Cottage
Cheese

tell me that you love me?

dreams about new love

Love that exists in glances and
first touches
Love that leaves everything else
unfinished
Love that leaves a stupid smile every
morning

Love that now exists only in dreams.

you know that I have really never loved

You crept
Into my bed
Late night
We laughed and spoke
Till the sun was above my head
And in those moments
We forgot
That we were over

nobody, but you

He whispered
Please. Don't go.
I stayed.
I shouldn't have.

I do my hair up, all high and wide

Drunk
I held on to your coat
We kissed.
In the rain. In Paris.
Drenched, I laughed
A stolen dream.
In a deserted street
Under a streetlight
Shivering in the cold.
We kissed.
In the rain. In Paris.

pink flamingo

Why do these words
Come pouring in
Early morning
Like an ache
That's long forgotten.

Do you like my fake nails daddy?

We didn't hold hands.
I climbed up on your shoulders
As you walked along the sea
A full moon night
While I swung my legs
Sitting pretty
Singing songs
Drumming your head
Absolutely in love.

Would you buy me a slice of cherry pie?

We got so high
I guess we did
not realise
Rose coloured lenses
Don't last forever

one, two

All the words were said to me
But never: You're Beautiful.
You walked in
And held me
As if it were always true.
As if it didn't matter
That no one
Had ever said them before

you look even more
handsome than you did the
day that I left you

Your love
Filled me up
And I never knew how
It felt before this.
It was too much.
Your love
Ruined me
And I never knew how
It hurt before this.
It was too much.
Your love
Tore me apart
And I never knew how
It broke before this.
It was too much
Your love.

how do you spend your nights, honey?

Pools of gold
Flooded the room
We were too busy
Feeling
touching
groping
You
me
us
Against
the
world

and other drugs

Was it love?
Or was it all the pills we took
Holding each other's face
Through blurred lines.
Pretending to be in films
Dancing to music
Only I could hear with you

come back to me, please

You and me
In circles
Love
Hurt
Hurt
Love
Tears and giggles
Why can't we
Walk away?

all I want is to feel good

You slept
I stared
Dreams do come true
If only I knew

come on now, if you want to

Stolen kisses
On the streets
Under blankets
In bars
Standing on tables
In cars
Hiding in rooms
Under tables
Over mountains

it's been a long time

I ran
Away
To you.
Your promises
Of keeping me safe
But why am
I running
Away
From you.

you know

Fairytales should not
Be told
To little girls
It fills their hearts
And breaks them

trash

I don't love
love anymore
I guess
I just can't
love things
that end with tears

magic

Snowflakes
We huddled close
Touched our toes
Snowflakes
You screamed with joy.
So ecstatic.
Slowly you grew tired
And bored
Snowflakes
Were not fun anymore.

the end

Past lovers
Like dreams that you
Want to remember
Want to forget
And you?
I wish I knew.